How to Say
Goodbye

How to Say Goodbye

THE WISDOM of HOSPICE CAREGIVERS

WENDY MacNAUGHTON

BLOOMSBURY PUBLISHING

NEW YORK • LONDON • OXFORD • NEW DELHI • SYDNEY

BLOOMSBURY PUBLISHING
Bloomsbury Publishing Inc.
1385 Broadway, New York, NY 10018, USA

BLOOMSBURY, BLOOMSBURY PUBLISHING,
and the Diana logo are trademarks of Bloomsbury Publishing Plc

First published in the United States 2023

Bloomsbury Publishing Plc does not have any control over, or responsibility
for, any third-party websites referred to or in this book. All internet addresses
given in this book were correct at the time of going to press. The author and
publisher regret any inconvenience caused if addresses have changed or sites
have ceased to exist, but can accept no responsibility for any such changes.

ISBN: HB: 978-1-63973-085-8; eBook: 978-1-63973-086-5

Library of Congress Cataloging-in-Publication Data is available

2 4 6 8 10 9 7 5 3

Printed and bound by Toppan Leefung Printing Ltd, China

Designed by Alvaro Villanueva

To find out more about our authors and books visit www.bloomsbury.com
and sign up for our newsletters.

Bloomsbury books may be purchased for business or promotional use. For
information on bulk purchases please contact Macmillan Corporate and
Premium Sales Department at specialmarkets@macmillan.com.

CONTENTS

FOREWORD

by BJ MILLER, MD

As a palliative care physician and friend, I have sat at the bedside of a lot of people who are dying. Old people. Young people. Angry people. Joyful people. Angry *and* joyful people. It's not always easy to die. And sometimes it's actually not that hard. Dying, like living, is much what you make of it.

What, somehow, seems consistently more difficult, and potentially transformative, is accompanying someone who is dying. Being the one at the bedside. Sitting at the edge of another's horizon. Now that is a doozy.

What I love about this book is that it is a distillation of that variable experience, not a reduction of it. There is a meaningful difference between distillation and reduction. Reduction is a Hallmark card, telling you to smile through your tears. Distillation is the pen, in this case Wendy's pen, choosing the signal from the noise.

Her drawings are homing beacons, inviting us to notice what we notice. To get out of our own way. To grapple with what is.

Presence, after all, is not an intellectual exercise. It's a corporeal surrender. Attuning, if you like. What does your body tell you about what the body before you is doing? What does your soul know about the one playing at the edge of existence right in front of you? Can you stop trying to figure *it* out and just be *it*?

I advise people to invest in aesthetics when people they love are dying—pay attention to the smells, sights, sounds, tastes—until the last possible moment. Because being alive is not about having a detectable pulse, but about having a detectable sense. Wendy's drawings are filled with this wisdom—the tea bag dipping into the hot water, the open mouth's labored breathing in sleep, the touch of a steady hand.

We are so poorly trained for this, my friends. We are taught to fix and verbalize, strategize and navigate. None of that will help you now. You can say some things, sure. In my experience, death *can be* a wonderful forcing function for loving, liberating conversations. And then again, sometimes the words feel flimsy. Or there are no words at all. In my humble opinion, we rely far too much on words in life. And are definitely failed by them in moments of reckoning with death. That's okay, Wendy reminds us. There are other languages—like art and attention, silence and super loud laughter. Showing up, too, is a language. Especially when someone is dying.

This book is not pretty. Pretty is strategic and tidy. This book is beautiful. Which is to say true. Death is like that: full of the sights and sounds and smells of dying, bodies doing bodily things. It's not always pretty. It's always beautiful.

May this book be a portal—a way for us to move beyond the unwise territory of trying to "do it right" and into the transcendent terrain of noticing what we can notice, loving who we love, and letting death—like life—surprise us with its ineffable beauty.

INTRODUCTION

Some years ago, I had the opportunity to be an artist-in-residence at the Zen Hospice Project, a six-bed residential facility situated in a light-filled house in San Francisco that, for thirty years until its closing in 2018, provided care for people at the end of their lives. I was in the house twice a week for nearly a year. During my time there, I witnessed nurses, aides, and volunteers care for the dying. More than just administering palliative aid and medication, the hospice caregivers created an atmosphere of compassion and helped the dying (and the people who love them) find peace in those final weeks, days, and hours of their life.

While there, I asked caregivers about their work: what it means to serve people at the end of their life. Why they do it. What they've learned through their experience. I sat with residents as they reflected on their lives and shared their feelings about death. And I wrote everything down. Meanwhile, I drew what I saw around the house and in the rooms of the people who were dying.

These drawings from inside the house, the words of the caregivers, and the pencil drawings I made of my own aunt Tildie drawn while she was dying under hospice care became the little book you hold in your hands.

I first created this as an artists' book, printing an edition of just two hundred. When I gave those copies away as gifts, I'd make a request: "If you find this little book helpful, please pass it on to someone else when they need it." Hearing stories of its usefulness to friends and strangers—and of its circulation through homes, therapist's offices, and hospitals—I decided to publish it more widely, this time with some perspective from hospice and palliative care physician BJ Miller and with a selection of additional resources.

Drawing is a way we can look closely at something we might otherwise be afraid to look at. I made this little book to help people, maybe you and certainly me, look closely at things that can feel scary, that we might otherwise avoid. For many of us, it's hard to know what to do when someone we love is dying—how to be, when to help, what to say. And though there isn't one right way to care for someone, hospice caregivers have experience we can all learn from. Their wisdom extends beyond the bedside.

Through caregivers at Zen Hospice, I learned about the "Five Things"—a framework for a conversation of love, respect, and closure. Variations on these five things have been written about and shared by many groups and cultures, I was told, including in a book by palliative care advocate Dr. Ira Byock.

While the book you're holding frames these Five Things as something to be shared with someone at the end of their life, this is a conversation we can have with our loved ones any time. Even after they're gone.

Caregivers often told me, "We are all dying. Our residents are just a little further along in the process." Death isn't something to be hidden or shied away from. Just the opposite. Dying is our greatest reminder to embrace the present and to deepen our relationships. At the end, that is all we have.

There is no one right way to say goodbye. My hope is this book can be a starting point.

—WENDY MACNAUGHTON

How to Say
Goodbye

IT'S VERY COURAGEOUS
to SIT with SOMEONE
WHILE THEY'RE DYING.

BUT YOU CAN'T ACTUALLY
DO ANYTHING.

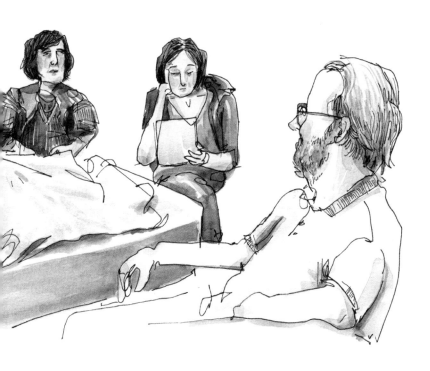

IT'S EASY to SAY,
"OKAY, HERE'S WHAT I WANT to DO.
HERE'S HOW I WANT IT to GO."

BUT YOU CAN'T FIX THIS.

YOU'RE NOT in CHARGE.

THE PERSON DYING IS in CHARGE.

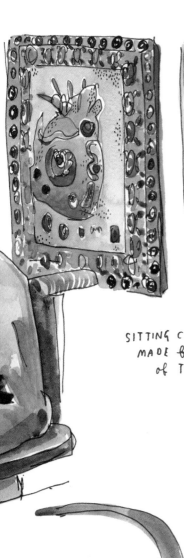

SITTING CLOSE to HER ARTWORK, PAINTINGS MADE from THOUSANDS and THOUSANDS of TINY BEADS.

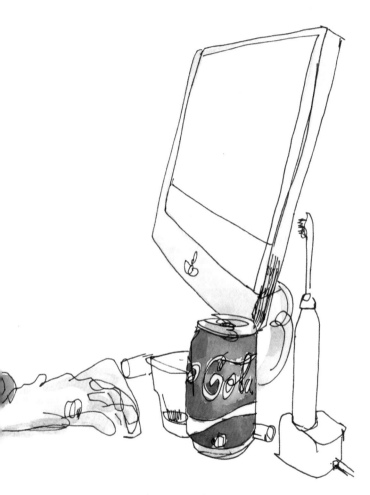

WRITING EMAILS to FAR AWAY FRIENDS
and TEACHING ME to SAY "FUCK OFF" in FRENCH.

KNITTING, SLEEPING,
REQUESTING BORSCHT for DINNER.

SOME PEOPLE ARE ORGANIZED and
WANT to SCHEDULE THINGS. THEY KNOW
EXACTLY HOW THE FUNERAL IS GOING
to BE, SET THINGS UP AHEAD of TIME.

OTHER FOLKS ARE in COMPLETE DENIAL
RIGHT UP UNTIL THE END.

EVERYONE HAS THEIR OWN VERSION
of WHAT A GOOD DEATH IS.
JUST LIKE EVERYONE HAS THEIR OWN
VERSION of WHAT MAKES A GOOD LIFE.

LET THE PERSON LEAD
THE CONVERSATION.

FOLLOW THEIR LEAD.

———————————————————

IF YOU DON'T KNOW WHAT to SAY,
START by SAYING THAT.

THAT'S VERY VULNERABLE.

SO MUCH FALLING AWAY.
THE BODY FALLING APART.

THERE'S A LOT GOING ON in
THAT CONVERSATION.

IT'S CURRENT.

RIGHT HERE.

RIGHT NOW.

NEITHER of YOU KNOWS WHAT to DO
in THIS SITUATION.

THAT OPENS THINGS UP.

The Five Things

THEY'RE HOW WE CAN
SAY GOODBYE.

I Forgive You.

Please Forgive Me.

Thank You.

I Love You.

Goodbye.

IF WE CAN HONESTLY SAY
THESE FIVE THINGS
WE CAN FEEL COMPLETE.

OUR LOVED ONES WILL KNOW
THERE IS NO UNFINISHED BUSINESS.

I Forgive You.

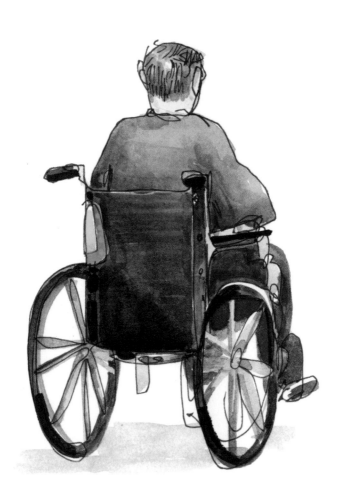

SIT in SILENCE.
IT'S OKAY to BE SILENT.

ALL ANYONE WANTS IS YOUR
PRESENCE and TO FEEL YOU'RE
PAYING ATTENTION.

WAITING for HER DAD to ARRIVE.

HOLD THEIR HAND.

Please Forgive Me.

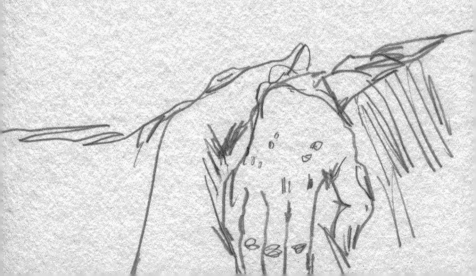

DON'T JUDGE YOURSELF.

ASK PEOPLE WHAT
THEY'D LIKE

and MAKE IT for THEM.

CONSIDER THE AESTHETICS.

ATTEND to THE DETAILS of THE SPACE.

ARRANGE THE ROOM.

THE SMELL of FOOD
COOKING in
THE KITCHEN

IT'S A SENSORY THING.

Thank You.

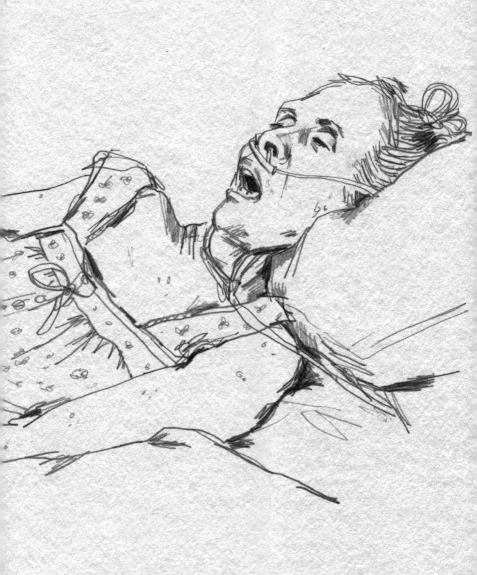

"THANK YOU" CAN LEAD to TALKING
ABOUT MEMORIES, SAYING,
"I REMEMBER WHEN..."

WATCHING.

SOMETIMES IT'S JUST
SITTING, and BEING THERE.

MANAGING PAIN KILLERS and MEDICATION.

PEOPLE ARE DIFFERENT DAY to DAY.
WITHIN ONE DAY,

THEIR MOOD CAN CHANGE.

THEIR ATTITUDE CAN CHANGE.

THEIR HEALTH CAN CHANGE.

GET COMFORTABLE
with CHANGE.

GET COMFORTABLE
with UNCERTAINTY.

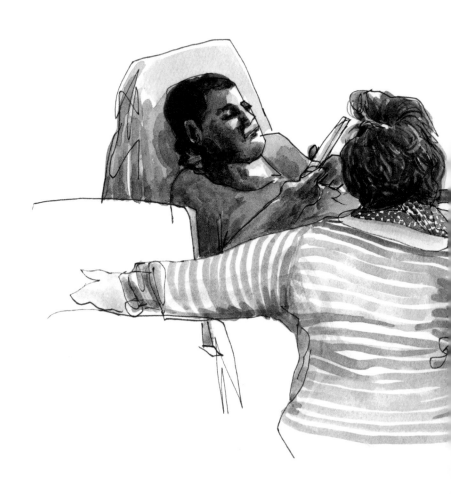

GET COMFORTABLE
with VULNERABILITY.

BE OPEN to
WHAT'S HAPPENING.

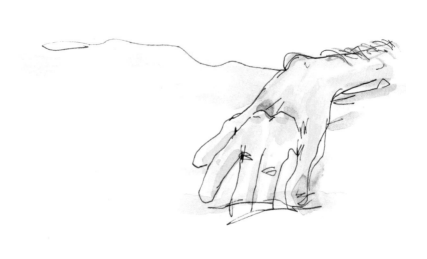

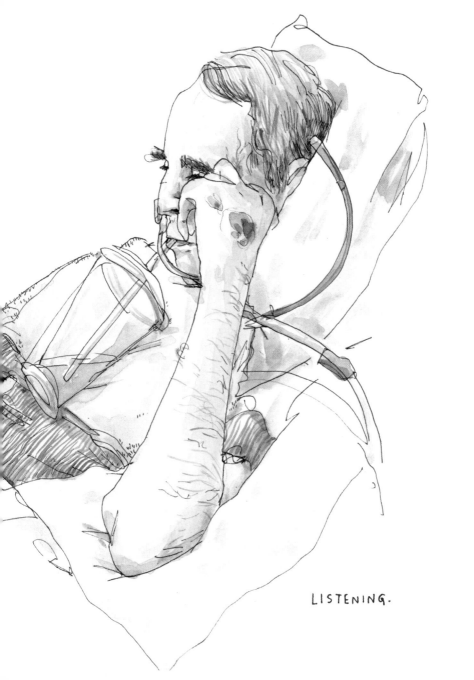

LISTENING.

CRY.

CRY A LOT.

I Love You.

LET IT UNFOLD.

LET IT HAPPEN.

SOMETHING SHIFTS WHEN
YOU DO THAT,

JUST BE THERE WITH THEM.

THAT'S ALL WE CAN DO.

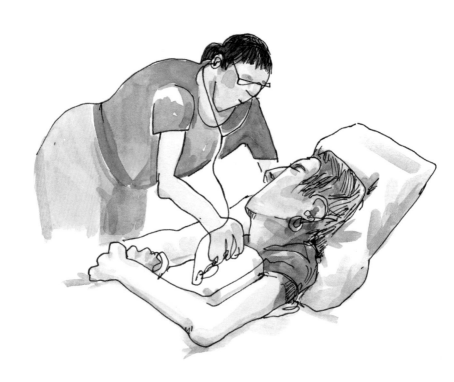

WAITING.

Goodbye.

THE END.

RESOURCES

While there's often nothing we can "do" when someone we love is dying, we may want to learn more about what to expect, how to navigate the process, and to connect with others who understand what we're going through.

Below are some books on caregiving, hospice, and palliative care that I found helpful while in residence at Zen Hospice Project, making the book you're holding, and after losing someone I loved. Most of the authors are leading doctors, social workers, and caregivers who have been at the bedside of thousands of people at the end of their life. Their wisdom is deep and lasting. Other authors are people who experienced loss firsthand and wanted to support others going through a similar process. You might recognize their words in your heart.

I've also included some organizations that could be helpful to people losing a loved one: resources for information and education for end-of-life support and caregiving. All of them are run by committed, caring experts.

Finally, there's a website called Prepare for Your Care. This is a place where *you* can create an advance care directive for your own death. This truly is something we can "do." By putting pieces in place for our own death, we lift difficult decisions off the shoulders of our loved ones. So when it's our turn to die, we help *them* say goodbye.

BOOKS

Being Mortal:
Medicine and What Matters in the End
Atul Gawande, MD
New York: Metropolitan Books, 2014

A Beginner's Guide to the End:
Practical Advice for Living life and Facing Death
BJ Miller, MD, and Shoshana Berger
New York: Simon & Schuster, 2019

The Four Things That Matter Most:
A Book About Living
Ira Byock, MD
New York: Atria Books, 2004

On Death and Dying:
What the Dying Have to Teach Doctors,
Nurses, Clergy & Their Own Families
Elisabeth Kübler-Ross, MD
New York: Simon & Schuster, 1969

The Five Invitations:
Discovering What Death Can Teach Us about Living Fully
Frank Ostaseski
New York: Flatiron Books, 2017

Being with Dying:
Cultivating Compassion and Fearlessness
in the Presence of Death
Roshi Joan Halifax
Boulder: Shambhala Publications, 2008

The Light of the World:
A Memoir
Eliabeth Alexander
New York: Grand Central Publishing, 2015

How We Die: Reflections on Life's Final Chapter
Sherwin B. Nuland
New York: A. A. Knopf, 1994

When Breath Becomes Air
Paul Kalanithi with Lucy Kalanithi
New York: Random House, 2016

Dying Well:
Peace and Possibilities at the End of Life
Ira Byock, MD
New York: Riverhead Books, 1997

Final Gifts:
Understanding the Special Awareness,
Needs, and Communications of the Dying
Maggie Callanan and Patricia Kelley
New York: Simon & Schuster, 2012

Modern Loss:
Candid Conversation about Grief. Beginners Welcome.
Rebecca Soffer and Gabrielle Birkner
Illustrated by Peter Arkle
New York: Harper Wave, 2018

Mettle Health

"Mettle Health provides support and guidance for individuals and families to live well in the face of health challenges, including consultations for patients and caregivers navigating a new diagnosis, a serious ongoing illness or end of life planning and grief."
mettlehealth.com

Zen Caregiving Project

(formerly Zen Hospice Project)
"Enhancing the experience of caregiving by teaching mindfulness and compassion."
zencaregiving.org

EndWell Project

"Education, support and inspiration when navigating end of life, grief and loss. They help ask the hard questions, share thought-provoking content and offers helpful resources that empower us to live fully until the end."
endwellproject.org

Inelda, International End-of-Life Doula Association
"An end-of-life doula guides a person who is transitioning to death and their loved ones through the dying process." Website offers information and resources on end-of-life doulas, including finding a doula and becoming a doula. inelda.org

MERI Center for Education in Palliative Care at UCSF/Mt. Zion
"Palliative Care seeks to provide support to people with serious illness at any stage of disease, whether their suffering is physical, emotional or spiritual." This MERI Center works to center the patient's wishes in their medical care through palliative care education. meri.ucsf.edu

Going with Grace
Founded by Alua Arthur, a death doula, attorney, and educator, the international organization Going with Grace offers training, courses, publications and community support for people planning for end of life— their loved ones or their own, and for people interested in becoming a death doula. goingwithgrace.com

Advance Care Directives

Prepare for Your Care
Easy-to-use website to create your own
advance care directives
(Available in both English and Spanish)
prepareforyourcare.org/

For Children

When a grown-up loses a loved one, there's probably a
young person experiencing loss, too. Children's books
that deal with death and loss can help start difficult conversations, answer questions, and identify and process
feelings. One chaplain's suggestion: if a child is losing a
parent, these books could be read to the child by a trusted
adult instead of the surviving parent. This offers a wider
circle of support to both the child and the parent.

CHILDREN'S BOOKS

The Tenth Good Thing about Barney
Written by Judith Viorst
Illustrated by Erik Blegvad
New York: Atheneum Books for Young Readers, 1971

Duck, Death and the Tulip
Written by Wolf Erlbruch
Wellington, NZ: Gecko Press, 2011

The Dead Bird
Written by Margaret Wise Brown
Illustrated by Christian Robinson
New York: HarperCollins, 2016 (new edition)

The Invisible String
Written by Patrice Karst
Illustrated by Joanne Lew-Vriethoff
New York: Little, Brown Books for Young Readers, 2018

The Fall of Freddie the Leaf: A Story of Life for All Ages
Written by Leo Buscaglia, PhD
Thorofare, NJ: SLACK Incorporated, 1982

The Heart and the Bottle
Written and illustrated by Oliver Jeffers
New York: Philomel Books, 2010

Charlotte's Web
Written by E. B. White
Illustrated by Garth Williams
New York: Harper & Brothers, 1952

Lifetimes: The Beautiful Way to Explain Death to Children
Writted by Bryan Mellonie
Illustrated by Robert Ingpen
New York: Bantam Books, 1983

Cry Heart, but Never Break
Written by Glenn Ringtved
Illustrated by Charlotte Pardi
Translated by Robert Moulthrop
New York: Enchanted Lion Books, 2016

Michael Rosen's Sad Book
Written by Michael Rosen
Illustrated by Quentin Blake
Somerville, MA: Candlewick Press, 2005

Badger's Parting Gifts
Written and illustrated by Susan Varley
New York: Lothrop, Lee & Shepard Books, 1984

Ida, Always
Written by Caron Levis
Illustrated by Charles Santoso
New York: Atheneum Books for Young Readers, 2016

CHILDREN'S ORGANIZATIONS

The National Alliance for Children's Grief (NACG) "raises awareness about the needs of children and teens who are grieving a death and provides education and resources for anyone who supports them." Website offers links to local resources and organizations throughout the United States. childrengrieve.org

ACKNOWLEDGMENTS

Thank you to the caregivers whose words comprise the text of this book: Roy Remer, Carlo Abruzzese, Derrick Guerra, Young Han, Lisa Katayama, MaryEllen Kirkpatrick, Grace Perez, Stan Stone, Kate Swan and Alistair Shanks. Thank you to the Zen Hospice Project (now Zen Caregiving Project), ZHP Guest House volunteers and kitchen staff, the Threshold Choir, and Ladybird Morgan, RN, MSW, CST, whose wisdom is present throughout.

My greatest respect and gratitude to the residents of the Guest House who trusted me to sit and draw them during their most vulnerable time of life: Billie, Jamaica, Jeanette, Jenny, Katherine, Patricia, and Russ, and to their families and loved ones. Thank you Ann Miller. And my own Aunt Tildie, whose portraits are rendered in graphite.

Thank you, Diane Mailey and Josh Kornbluth for making this artist's residency possible. And a deep thank you to BJ Miller for sharing your wisdom and heart in the foreword of this book. BJ was leading ZHP when I entered the Guest House and began this project. He created an environment where creative, unexpected things like this could take place. And while nothing stays forever, its seeds have scattered around the world.

Thank you to my beloved agent, Charlotte Sheedy, and to my editor, Nancy Miller, for always trusting and championing my work—it's an honor to work with you, Patti Ratchford, Katya Mezhibovskaya, Laura Phillips, and everyone at Bloomsbury. My dream team. Alvaro Villanueva designed both the artists' book and the book you hold in your hands. This would be a folder of files without his brilliant design mind. Thank you April Walters for early production assistance and thought partnership.

Thank you, Caroline Paul and Courtney Martin, Jon Mooallem, Wandee Pryor, Chris Colin, Maria Popova, Liz Ogbu, Anne Wintroub, Mike Birbiglia, Molly Ditmore, Rebecca Solnit, Andy and Linda Ach, and my parents, Robin and Candy MacNaughton.

This book is dedicated to Caroline Paul, without whom it, nor much of anything good really, would exist.

XX

A NOTE on THE ARTIST

Wendy MacNaughton is a *New York Times*-bestselling artist, illustrator, and graphic journalist with a degree in social work. Her work combines these practices to tell the stories of overlooked people and places, and uses drawing as a vehicle to connect people with one another and the world. She has illustrated and/or authored eleven books, including *Salt Fat Acid Heat* by Samin Nosrat and *The Gutsy Girl* by Caroline Paul. Her ongoing series of drawn journalism, Meanwhile, was the *New York Times*'s first weekly graphic journalism column. MacNaughton is the creator and host of DrawTogether, a social-emotional drawing program for kids, and the co-founder of Women Who Draw. She lives in the San Francisco Bay Area.